REL_ASING
FEAR

BY LIZ ADAMSON

THE ULTIMATE GUIDES
TO EMOTIONAL FREEDOM.

RELEASING FEAR
BY LIZ ADAMSON

Optimal Living Publications
Tel 01732-810430
Website: optimallivinginstitute.co.uk
Email: liz@edenbook.co.uk

ISBN 1-905759-11-8
1st Edition
Cover image by Di Frost

FEAR

Fear is the most destructive force there is in existence. It is at the root of virtually every problem or issue that we have to contend with in life. It affects everyone in varying degrees. Fear is always behind man's inhumanity to man. Our primary purpose on Earth is to overcome fear in its many guises and to instate love in its place. Fear creates hell on Earth and love will manifest Heaven. In this book we will look at fear, how it shows itself and affects us and practical ways in which we can eradicate it from our lives forever.

WHAT IS FEAR

FEAR IS A PROJECTION INTO THE FUTURE ABOUT SOMETHING THAT HAS ALREADY HAPPENED IN THE PAST.

We all have an individual cocktail of fears. These will depend on the experiences that we have had in the past; some fears come out of situations or traumas that have actually happened to us, while others may be learned. For instance, a child may develop a fear of heights because it fell off a table or down the stairs as an infant. This same fear may have been relayed to the child by the mother's reaction to it standing on the table or at the top of the stairs. We are not aware of the extent to which fear is inherited. Many parents pass on totally irrational fears like that of spiders. To a baby or child, its parents are strong and invincible, so if they are frightened there must be a good reason for it.

Once a fear is in place there are complex physical and emotional reactions that occur each time a fear is activated. The body prepares us for "fight or flight" in order to deal with the crisis. Our heart rate goes up, adrenaline is released into the body, we are alert, and our senses are heightened to help find a way out of our dilemma. In most cases the fear we are feeling is for something that has not actually happened. It is the anticipation of something that could happen. However, we respond to it as if the thing has actually occurred. Each time we feel fear we reinforce the belief that the cause of the fear is real.

In reality each experience we have is there to help us evolve and grow. If we do not like the outcome of a situation, we have learned the important lesson that we do not repeat the thought, belief or action that created that outcome. If we were to use this understanding in our growth, we would soon learn to evict all behaviours that do not serve us or tally with who or what we want to be. Fear prevents us from learning and growing in this way. It tells us that we are powerless victims and if something we did not like has happened to us once, it is likely to happen again. Fear blocks us from knowing that we are the creators of our lives and responsible for what we manifest.

Fear can totally paralyse us, especially when there is no genuine cause for the feeling. We find more things to be afraid of to explain the fear. We may then limit our lives to lessen any chance of coming into contact with the many triggers for fear. This may be so extreme in some cases that the only time these people are without fear is in their own homes with their loved ones safe around them.

Many of our fears lie dormant within the unconscious part of ourselves most of the time. It is only when something triggers them that they come to the surface and to our attention. Sometimes we may not be aware of the trigger or the source of the fear. As a child I became frightened of pygmies after watching a Sherlock Holmes drama on television. I used to get my brother to check under my bed for pygmies. Even now the word will set off a mild reaction, despite the fact that I know that they pose no threat to me and I am extremely unlikely to ever meet one. Once a fear surfaces, it will often feed off itself and grow out of all proportion. We might even get so caught up with the fear that we lose sight of what it was all about in the first place.

WHY DOES FEAR EXIST?

Fear has had a very important role to play in our evolution. If we are to grow and evolve consciously we have to experience all of life in order to be able to choose who and what we want to be and do. We live on a planet of duality. For every force there is an equal opposite force for there to be balance. There is up and down, right and left, good and bad and love and fear. In order to know one we have to experience the other. How would we know what hot is like if we could not compare it to cold? In the same way we cannot know love if we have not experienced fear and to choose love is our primary objective in life. Therefore learning about fear is an important aspect of this whole process.

The mass consciousness on this planet has become totally bogged down by fear, so much so that love is a concept that people are aware of and bandy the word around but few are genuinely familiar with on a constant basis. Even when we think we have found love in a relationship or from a child, parent or friend, fear will often step in. What if they leave me? What if they die? What if I can't take care of them or protect them well enough? The fears that surround love are endless.

There is another purpose for fear that was very important for the evolution of man. In order to survive it was necessary for *homo sapiens* to have fear for the things that would threaten his survival. These would include wild animals, extremes of weather, starvation and accidents. Fear of death or pain might be the thing that stops us from walking off a cliff or into a fire. Fear also sets up important physical changes in the body that allows us to deal with potentially dangerous situations.

However, when man had evolved enough to protect himself from nature and animals, fear had already taken hold and man had to find something else to project this fear onto. The only candidates became other men and God. God was perceived as a vengeful entity delivering disease, plagues and natural disasters. We then created the belief that other men would want to take what was ours: our self-esteem, our possessions, our spouses and our lives. As we have increased in number and sophistication, we have found more things to fear. It is interesting to note that as we have found more ways to protect ourselves, our fear has increased.

FEAR IS AN ILLUSION

The great irony of life is that fear and all its byproducts are an illusion. Most of the world is living and acting out this illusion for a majority of the time.

We often refer to fear as the shadow aspect and this is a good analogy. Shadow is simply an absence of light. It is not real. As soon as light is put onto the shadow, it disappears and we can see that there was in fact nothing there. Fear is an absence of love and as soon as love or one of its side effects is brought into the equation, the fear disappears and we can clearly see that it never existed.

RELEASING FEAR

Fear is always about something that may or may not happen in the future based on our past experience. Our reality is always in this moment and it is constantly changing. In this second the thing we are afraid of is not happening. On the rare occasions that we do find ourselves in challenging situations, we are usually too busy dealing with them to feel fear. If we do feel afraid it is often more about the outcome of the situation. "What if I die?" "What if I fail this exam?" "What if I don't get this job?"

Sometimes fear will only set in as a reaction once the danger or difficulty has passed. This came home to me when I was attacked in the middle of the night in my flat. While the intruder was there, I was so busy surviving, it was only when he left that there was room for the fear to emerge. I then spent the next six months being afraid even though I was perfectly safe.

We are so powerful that we can create something that does not exist. We are taught how to fear and what to fear and we then see endless instances that reinforce our fear and give us the tangible evidence that we need to justify it.

RELEASING FEAR

It is essential that we acknowledge fear as the illusion that it is if we are to eliminate it and its destructive side effects from our lives.

HOW FEAR MANIFESTS

We can all associate with the experience and feeling of fear. We might feel it before an exam or if we hear strange noises in the night. What might not be quite so clear is that fear is at the source of every single negative thought, word or deed in the world. The byproducts of fear are often more prominent than the fear itself. Some of the many manifestations are as follows:

Worry and doubt - fear put into thoughts and words.
Anger and aggression - fear put into action.
Guilt   - fear that we are not
          enough and should be
          punished for it.
Greed and avarice - fear that there is not enough.

RELEASING FEAR

Judgement	)	- fear that we are not enough.
Criticism	)	we need to make others less
Prejudice	)	to feel better about ourselves.
Jealousy	)	- fear that others have more than
Envy	)	us.
Control		- fear of not getting needs met.
Competitiveness		- fear of failure.
Limitation		- fear of powerlessness.
Struggle		- fear that we do not deserve to thrive
Loss		- fear that man or God will take what is ours

Out of these manifestations of fear come all the problems that are affecting and destroying the earth at this time. Disease, wars, ecological problems, famine, pollution, violence and racism to name a few. Each person plays a part in creating these situations by entertaining fear in their lives.

FEAR THAT WE ARE NOT GOOD ENOUGH

We can see from the various ways in which fear manifests that a core belief runs through much of our fear and that is that we are not good enough. This belief alone motivates most of our actions. We are determined to prove to others and even ourselves that we are good enough by achieving, succeeding, having or being more than others. At the other end of the spectrum, we may be victimised, abused, down-trodden or marginalised because we do not believe we deserve any more than this. It is important to note that those with a confident or even arrogant exterior will usually have big issues about not being good enough. It is what I call inferiority masquerading as superiority.

The belief that we are not good enough is imprinted onto us at a very early age. For a start, we probably have parents who do not feel good enough about themselves. Very few babies and children consistently get their needs met. Under five year olds think that the world revolves around them, therefore they are not good enough to get their needs met. Once this understanding is lodged, life will consistently reinforce it right into adulthood and beyond.

Our underlying belief that we are not enough will show itself in many different ways. We may be demanding, aggressive, manipulative, greedy, power hungry, controlling or judgmental. Equally, we may be very selfless and giving, trying to meet everyone else's needs in the hope that they will take their cue from us and give back what we have put out. Sadly, this rarely occurs.

It is essential in releasing fear that we remove the belief that we are not enough or undeserving of all the rich bounty that life on this planet has to offer.

FEAR AND ANGER

I will be addressing some of the main manifestations of fear individually. Anger is one of the most prominent of these. Anger is usually aimed at a person and will occur when we are thwarted in getting our needs and desires met. Once again, at the root of this is the fear that we are not enough. An infant that does not get its food, attention, treats or is thwarted in any way may react angrily to the situation. When the child grows up, the needs may be different but the anger is the same if our desires are denied.

Anger is a very strong and powerful emotion and for many it is more acceptable to feel and express anger than fear. Fear appears to be weak and powerless. Anger will often engender fear in others and it may seem preferable to see this fear and be the perpetrator of it rather than admit to our own fears.

Anger puts a very strong barrier between us and the rest of the world. This effectively keeps people out and unable to get close to us. This may appear to protect us from our fear of being hurt. The theory is that we cannot be hurt if we don't let people in. However, the rejection, isolation and loneliness we experience as a result of our anger will end up hurting us anyway.

Fear is an emotion that is often internalised but when it is expressed as anger, it becomes externalised and active. Our anger will often impact on other people or things and if left unchecked can be extremely destructive.

FEAR AND PAIN

At the end of the day most of our fears can be classed as fear of pain. Some of these fears will involve physical pain and others emotional. Fear of heights, snakes and attack come into the former category. However, our fears of emotional pain are often predominant. It comes in many different guises. Fear of rejection, ridicule, criticism and failure are just a few of the things that we may commonly fear that will cause us pain.

Many aspects of our lives may be governed by our trying to avoid feeling pain. This will depend greatly on the degree to which we have experienced pain in the past. Those who have had a difficult childhood may avoid getting close to people for fear that they will hurt them.

Fear of hurt will often affect us most within the arena of relationships. We may look to our partners to make up for all the things that we did not get in childhood or the perceived hurts that were created. When our partner inevitably fails to do this, we feel hurt, rejected and let down and we emotionally or physically withdraw from the relationship. Once we see that being close to people has such a potential for hurt, we become very wary of opening ourselves and our hearts within relationships. This is the one prerequisite needed for a successful partnership, without it we relate on a very superficial level or find that we split up before there is any intimacy in the union.

RELEASING FEAR

There is one particular pattern of behaviour that has emerged out of our fear of hurt that is very destructive. It is our need to protect ourselves by hurting others before they can hurt us or "get them before they get you." This situation will always arise out of our own pain from the past. When we employ this mode of behaviour, one of two situations will occur. We either become a bully or a tyrant who chooses to hurt people who will not fight back or the objects of our taunts will give as good as they get or better and we become the targets for their attack. Whichever scenario we choose will end up creating the very situation that we were protecting ourselves against, namely hurt. The solution to this issue is to change the "Get them before they get you." philosophy to "Do unto others as you would be done by."

There is another way of deactivating the hurt we have taken on and safeguarding us from being hurt in the future and that is by not taking the words or actions of others personally. Anytime anyone says or does something that is hurtful, it is never about us, it is always about them. If we detach from the situation and choose to see that it is not our problem but theirs, there is no reason to be hurt again. We can then go through life with an open heart and a compassionate mind.

Our fear of hurt is often deeply ingrained and works on an unconscious level. People who seem to be least prone to being hurt will often have the deepest fear of it. They have merely employed very strong protective and defensive mechanisms that are designed to hide any hurt or vulnerability lying behind them.

It is important to notice how our fear of being hurt limits us in our lives. Do we keep ourselves small and invisible for fear of judgement and criticism? Do we do jobs that offer little growth or challenge for fear of rejection or failure? Do we act like sheep and follow any trends that are set rather than choosing to be the individual we are for fear of ridicule or humiliation? Do we do dangerous or destructive things in order to be accepted by our peer group? It takes a brave person to stand up and live his life authentically and up to his potential. If we can find the courage to do this, it will set us free.

FEAR OF LOSS

Many of the fears that we have are centred around loss. These losses may occur in many different areas. It could be loss of a loved one, loss of property, a job, money or status, loss of dignity or even loss of ones own life.

When we have a fear of losing something, we often cling onto it or protect it from who or what might threaten it. When we do this to people or situations, we sometimes end up creating the very scenario that we were guarding against in the first place.

One of the most liberating concepts we can take on board is that there is nothing that we can lose or may be taken away from us that we cannot either replace or acknowledge is making way for something new or better to come along. This would even include our own lives. This may be a difficult belief to entertain. It involves totally going with the flow and ebb of life. It demands complete acceptance of everything that happens to us and the discipline to look for and find the silver lining or gift in every challenging situation.

Fear of loss once again is anticipating something that has not yet happened. Many of the losses we fear are inevitable, like the death of parents, family members and pets or children growing up and leaving home. When we live in dread of these things, we are unable to enjoy what is on offer while they are around. I had a friend who would get into a huge state of fear about her parents dying. Every time she would see them she would imagine her life when they were gone and she would often cry all the way home from a visit. These parents were hale and hearty and probably had many good years left in them that she was ruining for herself.

RELEASING FEAR

When we put too much emphasis on the material world, we lay ourselves open to the fear of losing the things that we put so much value onto. Once again, we are unable to enjoy them or share them with others who might appreciate them. We may even keep them locked up in banks or safes so that they would not be lost to us. We are simply the caretakers of property, paintings, furniture and jewels. When we have done our stint, we pass the job onto someone else.

FEAR AND WORRY

Worry is one of the most prevalent forms of fear. We all experience worry from time to time and there are some people who have turned it into an art form.

We will worry about things that have either not yet happened or that we are powerless to do anything about. This is why worry is a complete waste of time and energy and prevents us from enjoying our existence at an optimal level. The vast majority of things we worry about never happen or are a figment of our imaginations. The things that do occur will be dealt with at the time. These include things like exams, job interviews, moving house etc. There will usually be an immediate sense of relief and satisfaction when these things are completed.

Note that there is a difference between being well prepared and organised and worrying. Worrying is all in the mind and rarely has any physical action attached to it. Worry will create a mild fear response in the body. Consequently, those who are prone to worry at night often find that they cannot sleep and will spend the time building on the initial worry. The heart rate increases, adrenaline is pumped through the body and we are alert to any potential dangers, not conditions that are conducive to a good nights sleep.

Many of us spend a great deal of time and effort worrying about what others think of us. We make assumptions as to why someone has not phoned or invited us round lately. We will usually come to completely the wrong conclusion and then behave as if this is true. We will often project our insecurities and weaknesses onto others, imagining that they are thinking about these things or gossiping to others about us. As soon as we can acknowledge that WHAT OTHER PEOPLE THINK OF US IS NONE OF OUR BUSINESS, we are free to be who we are and not worry about how others choose to perceive us.

Trust is the antidote to fear and worry and we need the discipline to instate it as part of our daily lives.

FEAR AND CONTROL

The need in people to control themselves, situations and others is always born out of fear. We think that as long as we are orchestrating everything in our lives, then we can avoid any pitfalls, pain or disappointment along the way.

RELEASING FEAR

This is an impossible situation. While we may be able to instate control over ourselves with a great deal of energy and discipline, we are not able to extend this to others or circumstances. This will reinforce a sense of powerlessness that in turn will increase the need for control. This very destructive cycle is self-perpetuating.

The areas where control will most often show itself will be in relationships, the family and the work place. These are also places where most misery can be created. In order for a person to be able to exert control over others, they must have a weapon to wield. This weapon will usually be fear or guilt.

Part of the control pattern is to whittle away at the self-esteem of the person being controlled. If we are told often enough that we are stupid, incompetent, ugly or unacceptable, we tend to believe it. Once we are rendered completely power-less, the controller is able to threaten us with the withdrawal of love, attention, financial support or our job. We believe that no one else would want to love, employ us, or even know us because this is what we have been told. Consequently, we usually end up giving in to the demands of the controller. A controller will often try to disconnect us from our support systems like family and friends that might undermine his position.

So called "control freaks" are probably the most fearful people there are. This is often very well camouflaged by the illusion of strength and power that these people exude.

In dealing with the issue of controlling people, we need to keep in mind that these people only have control over us if we choose to give it to them. If we do not give into the fear then they are powerless to do anything. Even if we lose the job or relationship, we are better off without it.

Controllers are usually created out of a child-hood where they were controlled or the victim of circumstances that were completely beyond their control. This may be the loss of a parent, constant moving, poverty, lack of love or many other issues. All of these situations will engender a great deal of fear that they do not want to repeat.

FEAR AND STRUGGLE

One of the best indications that we are entertaining fear in our lives is struggle. If we seem to be expending huge amounts of energy and at the end of the day we are still at the same place, we are in struggle. If life is about survival and simply existing, then we are in struggle. If we are tired, lacking in joy, fun and abundance, then we are in struggle. If we are robotically going through a daily cycle of sleeping, working, eating and watching television, then we are in struggle.

The fact is that struggle has become so much a part of normal human living that we fail to recognise the epidemic that it is. If we see everyone else struggling to get from A to B, doing work that they don't enjoy just to survive, in relationships that do not fulfil them or struggling to find one at all or stressed to the eyeballs from trying to juggle so many things, we do not question it. This seems to be how life is and we have to get on with it. STRUGGLE IS NOT NATURAL BUT IT HAS BECOME NORMAL. We have to begin to buck the trend and give up struggle as a way of life.

Struggle occurs when we go against the natural flow of life. It is the ego that feeds us the fear that perpetuates this. It is as if most of humanity is swimming upstream. Only those who are very strong, hard working and determined will make much headway here but in the wrong direction. Occasionally we come across someone who is floating on his back, going with the current and with a big smile on his face. The ego and society will often condemn or ridicule these people, they are weirdos, dropouts and subversives and should not be followed under any circumstances. They are mocked and laughed at, but who is the one that is laughing?

GOING WITH THE FLOW may be a very hackneyed expression but it is the only way to eliminate struggle in our lives. When we go with the flow, we are in a complete state of trust and acceptance. We do not know what lies around the next bend but we do know it will be wonderful, there will be gifts, miracles, abundance, synchronicity, opportunity and growth.

It is impossible not to fulfil our destiny and potential if we are moving in the right direction. It is almost a given.

There are many fears that stop us from going against the struggling tide of humanity. We are afraid to be different, afraid of judgments, criticism and ridicule, afraid of being unacceptable or ostracised, afraid of rejection and persecution, afraid of losing our friends, family and status, afraid of the unknown. These fears are all illusions. The rewards for going with the flow are unlimited. It will only take a small percentage of people willing to give up the fear, struggle, hardship and lack to completely turn the tide for everyone else. Very soon people will be doing U turns in their droves and realising the benefits of doing so. The time to do this is NOW.

FEAR AND THE EGO

The ego plays a huge part in presenting our fears to us in many different guises. The ego is that very destructive voice in our minds that feed us all our negative or critical beliefs, thoughts and feelings.

When the ego is in control of our lives, things will either be chaotic or totally stagnant and this is because the main energy the ego works with is fear. It is the voice that gives us the "what ifs...." , it tells us that we are not good enough, not deserving etc.

The ego is like a parasite that feeds off us, it is not who we are. When the host allows the parasite to keep on growing, it ends up taking over, using up all the nutrients and energy until the host is all but swallowed up by it. This is what we unconsciously are letting happen with the ego. We allow it and the fear it works with to completely overshadow our true and loving selves and we constantly feed it and reinforce it with our energy and power.

If we do not give our power to the ego, then fear

would have no affect on our lives and we would be free. We give power to fear and the ego every time we believe the propaganda that it delivers and when we live the illusion as if it were real.

I do not believe in evil as a concept. I simply see people who appear to be wicked as those who have a huge amount of fear and are working totally from an ego perspective. In any given moment, we are allowing either love and the inner Divine or fear and the ego to sponsor us. One will deliver joy, fun and miracles and the other pain, suffering and struggle.

The ego is totally assertive and if we are not consciously deciding what we want to think and believe, then the ego will come in with its fear, guilt, hurt, judgements and control. Sadly, most of the world is living unconsciously and unaware that there is a choice, so the ego is able to run amok unchecked.

The ego will often disguise itself as our best friend who wants to protect and take care of us. It will present our fears in a way that is very nurturing. It will say things like "you don't want to leave your low paid, dead end job because you know you mess up interviews with your nerves and you can't handle rejection anyway. You are fine where you are." If we believe these things, then we will stay stuck and in struggle. Instead, we need to listen to the voice of our intuition that will give us precise instructions as to our destiny.

The positive aspect of the ego is that it is only able to feed us fears that we actually have already. We can therefore use this information to eliminate fear from our lives altogether. We do this by making use of the information that the ego provides us in showing us the unhealed illusions of fear that we are holding onto and manifesting. More of this in part two.

FEAR AND POWER

Power is a very emotive word and we probably have many different concepts of it. Some people want it and go to great lengths to try and achieve it. Others are afraid of it and avoid any opportunity to exercise it.

For me there are two types of power, external or ego power and internal Divine power. Those who do not experience any of the latter may try to access power from the former. Equally those in touch with their inner power have no need to look for it elsewhere. External power is usually created through success, money, status and position. It is often created at the expense of and by disempowering others. Internal power conversely is available to absolutely everyone and it is increased by empowering others.

When we are in a state of fear, we are completely powerless. We give our power away to the fear or to the person wielding it and that leaves us with no resources to dispel the illusion. Anything we give power and energy to will expand, even if it never existed in reality in the first place. It is our power that gives it life and our continued feeding of it will turn it into a monster that will seem too big to handle.

It is important to note that no one or nothing is capable of taking our power, we can only give it away. The good news is that once it is given it is a simple process to take it back. We are not stuck with being powerless. We do need to have the awareness to recognise how and when we are handing it over.

When we are in touch with our inner power, we take responsibility for what we create and manifest, no matter what it is. When we do not do this, we become victims. We see everything that happens to us as being due to what others or circumstances do to us and we are powerless. A victim is often riddled with fear and will attract destructive people and situations to them as a result.

When we are truly in touch with our personal power there is no room for fear.

FEAR IS A MAGNET

There is a Universal law of attraction that states that we attract to us what we are putting out. This is particularly true in the case of fear as this is a very strong vibration. Whatever fears we have will draw to us the very thing we most dread. For instance, if we fear rejection or criticism, these things will probably play a large part in our lives.

We have all have heard of people who have been burgled countless times while their neighbours have got away scot free. Each burglary will increase the amount of fear around the occupants and consequently attracts further break ins.

There was a period in my life where I was in a great deal of fear. During this time I had what I called "the disaster of the day." These disasters included car trouble, a fire, a bomb scare, a couple of burglaries, fraud and embezzlement. All of these things were apparently beyond my control and power and yet I know it was my fear that magnetised them to me. As soon as the fear was dissipated, the disasters no longer occurred.

There can also be a group consciousness of fear that can draw negative energies to particular countries or issues. An example of this occurred after the Sept 11 disasters. A huge amount of fear was focussed on flying and planes. In the following few months there were five bad plane crashes that had nothing to do with terrorism. Each person who feels fear is contributing to the mass pool that can result in attracting the very thing they fear most.

FEAR AND LACK

Many of our fears centre around scarcity and lack, particularly in terms of money and the material. These fears are not just limited to times when we do not have enough. Redundancy, marriage break ups, lack of promotion, economic recession and unemployment are all spectres that may haunt us from time to time.

RELEASING FEAR

A large proportion of people stay in jobs that they actively dislike because they perceive this to be the only way to feed, clothe and shelter themselves and their families. They do not believe that the universe would support them in doing what they love and still have enough for all their needs. Some brave people do try and give it up to live their dreams but any fear or belief in lack will create struggle and failure, which reinforces the understanding that we cannot do and have what we want.

When we worry about finances, we will often be powerless and passive, this will in turn block us from finding and acting upon the solution to our predicament. For every situation there is a perfect remedy available, we have simply to seek it.

It is really important not to get into the habit of focussing on lack and what we can't afford. By changing our perception to one of abundance, given the same circumstances, we will then attract this into our lives.

Conversely, it is important to note that fear of

lack is often the motivating force behind many very materially successful and wealthy people. However, the downside of this is that material gain does not remove the fear, so no matter how much they have, it is never going to be enough to make them feel secure.

Trust is always going to be the antidote to money worries. We might not know what the solution is going to be but it will always be presented in the perfect moment.

SIGNS OF FEAR

There may be many indications that fear is playing a large and destructive part in our lives. We may not always be aware that fear is at the root of these things.

Some of these signs are:
1) Panic attacks.
2) Waking up in the night or early morning and not being able to go back to sleep.

RELEASING FEAR

3) Waiting for the bad news. Dreading the arrival of the post or the phone ringing.

4) The inability to feel happy or joyful, feeling like a dark cloud is following you everywhere you go.

5) In a constant state of struggle and stress.

6) Feeling victimised and powerless.

7) Trying to control people and situations.

8) An unwillingness to take risks or try anything untried or tested.

9) Seeming to be plagued with bad luck.

10) Pessimism.

11) Being aggressive as a means of protection.

12) Avoiding situations or people who may challenge us.

13) Being in a state of scarcity and lack.

14) Procrastination.

THE SPECTRUM OF FEAR

Fear covers a large spectrum of feeling and it may not always be obvious that what we are feeling is fear. At the lower end of the spectrum we may experience nervousness, anxiety, worry and doubt. These feelings tend to be ongoing and about rather general everyday things that are beyond our control to deal with.

At the upper end of the scale are feelings of panic, alarm, fright, horror and terror. These much stronger feelings will usually appear in response to a specific stimulus. This could be anything from a loud bang to the presence of an axe murderer. These feelings will usually only last as long as the catalyst for them is there. In these circumstances the body is geared for the fight or flight response in order to deal with the problem.

When we have had experiences that have created the more powerful feelings of fear this will often leave a legacy of low grade fear. It may be necessary to go back and discharge the feelings from whatever incidents have created the fear so that there is no residue to be dealt with at a later date.

FEAR IS A CHOICE

In any given moment we are either choosing fear or love. Most of the time this is an unconscious, passive choice. Each day we have tens of thousands of thoughts going through our heads. The vast majority of these we are not consciously aware of. If we ask someone the last thought they had, they would probably not be able to remember it. Every single one of those thoughts has a charge of love or fear and this charge serves to attract to us and create just what we were thinking about. It is well within our ability to control whether we create positive or negative situations. To do this we have to become conscious, to raise our consciousness and awareness. If we choose, we can put a love charge onto everything we think and do and then there is nothing that we cannot be, do or have in our lives. The choice is ours to make.

FEAR AND PHOBIAS

The nature of fear is such that once it has been established there will be an unconscious reaction that occurs every time the particular stimulus is around. We will then feed the fear with our energy and blow the situation out of all proportion. Most things we are frightened of will usually not be capable of hurting us in any way or only in extreme circumstances.

In dealing with phobias we need to have an understanding of the unconscious mind. It is not able to rationalise for itself the level of actual danger that is posed by anything we may encounter. The unconscious will merely record the thoughts, feelings and beliefs about what we experience. When we come up against the same thing or situation, the unconscious will bring up from its memory bank our complete reaction and we will feel and think the same things as before, all the while adding more fear to the equation in the process.

In dealing with phobias it is essential to undo the unconscious programming that created the fear. It may be necessary to go back to the source of the phobia and dissipate the fear response here. As soon as the unconscious is programmed for a different response to the stimulus, the phobia does not exist.

If left untreated a phobia can completely dominate our lives. We are always looking ahead for any possibility of the stimulus being present. We limit ourselves and avoid any situation where there is any chance of an encounter. We may exercise our imaginations and visualise the experience even when it is not occurring. We may also drag our nearest and dearest into the equation and limit them or expect them to shield us from our fears. This is too great a burden to put on some people and it may end up alienating them. Many relationships break up as a result.

Sometimes we are not always willing to give up

our fears or phobias. There may be a big pay off that we are hanging onto. Not everyone is consciously aware of this. When we do not have to put ourselves to the test and find out if we are going to fail or succeed in the things we try. When our fear forces others to take care of us or to be responsible for our lives. When we do not have to go out in the world or earn our own living, we can always imagine or fantasise about who we could be without facing the reality.

ᵽANIC ATTACKS

Panic or anxiety attacks are becoming increasingly common in our society. They are very closely related to phobias in that the physical response is very similar. The major way in which they differ is that they are not created in response to a specific stimulus. It is often very hard to pinpoint what has triggered the attack. Consequently, the sufferer will focus more strongly on the physical symptoms rather than the cause. These symptoms are the things that are most frightening. The heart rate increases and there may be pain in the chest area that feels to the victim like a heart attack. The inability to breathe is another symptom that makes some people feel as if they are going to die. There may be a fear of blacking out but this very rarely happens.

The humiliation of having an attack in public plays a huge part in the misery of panic attacks and will often limit the number of places that the sufferer feels safe to go.

The inability to pinpoint the source of the fear is a huge aspect of the problem with panic attacks. The unconscious fear response will often acknowledge the place or situation where the panic attack occurred in the past and reactivate the fear in similar circumstances. So if an attack occurred in a supermarket, on a bus or train, these will become no go areas. Severe sufferers may get to a point where everything becomes a potential trigger and they become prisoners in their own homes.

Control is often a big issue within panic attacks.

It is felt that if that person is in control of every aspect of their lives and environment, then the attacks may be warded off. Unfortunately, when this control extends to other people and their actions, it is not always welcomed and this will isolate the sufferer still further.

Panic attacks are a severe problem that if not addressed can completely take over our lives and keep us totally stuck. The fear experienced is a complete illusion and yet it is real in every physical sense. It is essential to get to the root of why the attacks are there. What was going on emotionally when they first occurred? What is the pay-off? Is there any hereditary or learned behaviour involved? It is very common for panic attacks to run in families.

The most important aspect of dealing with panic attacks is to find the tools to deal with the feelings when they arise and not by reinforcing them by avoiding any people or places where they have occurred before.

FEAR AND CHILDREN

It is essential that we do not teach children to be fearful. Many fears and phobias are learned from the family and those around in childhood. This does not mean that babies and children are not made aware of potential dangers and how to deal with them but that fear is not an element that is brought into the teaching.

If a child is taught that by touching some thing hot, it will be burnt and this hurts, we do not want it to be afraid of the fire, stove or iron. We want a child to learn the consequences of its actions. This puts the situation completely under its power and control. If we do not want the consequences of pain, then we learn not to repeat the action that created it. The lesson is as simple as that and does not need to involve any fear.

Many people believe that a bit of fear is a good thing in bringing up children. If we are frightened of our parents or teachers, we will be obedient and well-behaved. While this may be true, the destruction created to the child's self-esteem and worth is enormous.

In the same way, many religions teach that we should fear God and that if we misbehave, his wrath and punishment will be visited down on us. Instead of this, we as adults can be made aware of the consequences of our thoughts, words and actions, without any taint of fear.

"WHAT IF...." SYNDROME

The "what if" syndrome is one of the most insidious forms of fear. We all participate in this to a greater or lesser extent. The situations where the "what ifs" occur are almost endless and they may appear out of the blue. A typical scenario would be if a loved one is late for an appointed meeting or coming home and we begin to think, "what if they have been involved in a horrific accident and are fighting for their lives?" Other "what ifs" might be. "What if I lose my job and I am unable to pay the mortgage and I am out on the street?" or "What if my husband leaves me and no one wants me and I end up alone?"

Once we start on a "what if", it usually does not stop there, we look at the consequences of that "what if" and begin to think, feel and act as if it were true. It is like a negative fantasy that builds on itself until we are almost convinced that it is real. Sometimes we actually feel the loss, hurt, anger or guilt that would result from the situation.

We need to be aware if we are "what if" addicts. A vast amount of our time and energy will be wasted on this fruitless pursuit. There is also a danger that we may thrive on the drama of the fantasies, seeing ourselves as the hapless victim waiting to be rescued. This is not a very healthy way of being.

When we indulge in constant "what ifs," we are putting the focus of our attention on the future and living in a reality that does not yet exist. Consequently, we are not living and enjoying what is happening in this moment.

The more creative and imaginative we are, the more detailed and real our "what ifs" will seem to be. The scenarios may be accompanied by technicolour pictures in our minds, which further reinforce the realism.

Some of the "what ifs" do happen in the real world. People do have horrific car accidents, are made redundant and marriages do break up. However, we are able to deal with these things if and when they occur and we will move on and other things will come into our lives. We are powerless to deal with a "what if" as it has not occurred and in all probability will never occur.

FEAR AND ILLNESS

When we have a great deal of fear that has not been processed, it will have a destructive affect on the physical body. Many ailments that we have will have fear at the root of the situation. Just as fear may play a significant part in creating illness, love will play a huge part in healing and releasing the problem. Typical ailments that fear contributes to are: digestive or bowel problems, joint problems, lung and breathing ailments.

FEAR FOR OTHERS

Many of our fears are not focussed on ourselves but on those who are nearest and dearest to us. Once again, this emphasises our powerlessness. We may be able to bring in protection mechanisms to ensure our own safely but we are unable to do this with others.

As we have already seen, some people deal with this by trying to control other people but usually others do not appreciate or allow this to happen.

We waste a huge amount of time worrying about other people. This may be a way of distracting ourselves from what is not working in our own lives. We focus on everyone else's problems rather than deal with our own.

When we accept that each individual is responsible for its own life and that the challenges that present themselves will ultimately contribute to the growth and evolution of the person, we can let go of any fears we have on their behalf.

FEAR AND EXCITEMENT

If we look at the physical feelings that manifest when we feel fear; sweaty palms, increased heart rate, butterflies in the stomach, we can see that these same symptoms also apply to the feeling of excitement.

Both fear and excitement anticipate some thing that may or may not happen in the future, one negatively and the other in a positive light.

Another positive manifestation of the fear feeling is thrill. When we go on a roller coaster, bungee jumping or throw ourselves from a plane, the feeling will be the same only some people perceive it as fear, while others choose to enjoy it and see it as a thrill.

It is up to us how we choose to feel and what kind of charge we project into our future. One will create good feelings while the other makes us feel bad.

TYPES OF FEAR

There are many different fears that affect us. Fear is not logical and many of the fears we have totally contradict each other. For instance, we may fear failure at the same time as fearing success. There are many fears that are common for most people. If we want to know what we are afraid of, we have only to look at our lives, it will tell us everything we need to know. Fears will show themselves in two ways. First, we will tend to attract to us people and situations that will reinforce our fears. Many of our unconscious patterns that have repeated again and again will contain our strongest fears. Secondly, we will consciously avoid people and situations that are likely to put us in a position of realising our fears. If we are afraid of rejection, we may not go into relationships where rejection could take place.

Some of the most common fears are listed below:

Fear of failure.
Fear of success.
Fear of not being good enough.
Fear of rejection.
Fear of abandonment.
Fear of power.
Fear of powerlessness.
Fear of scarcity and lack.
Fear of commitment.
Fear of attack.
Fear of authority.
Fear of being excluded.
Fear of ridicule and humiliation.
Fear of intimacy.
Fear of being judged.

RELEASING FEAR

Fear of being out of control.
Fear of being stupid and boring.
Fear of change.
Fear of death. (your own or others)
Fear of loss.
Fear of invasion.
Fear of madness.
Fear of not being accepted.
Fear of pain.
Fear of being vulnerable.
Fear of people.
Fear of the unknown.

I have not included any of the common phobias on this list since they are simply the symptoms or triggers for other fears.

DEALING WITH AND RELEASING FEAR.

RELEASING FEAR

In our quest for a fear free life, we need to approach the issue in two different ways. First, we need to have strategies and tools to hand to deal with fear as and when it shows itself. Secondly, we can remove the triggers and the unconscious fears that feed virtually all our destructive behaviour. In part two of this book I give practical methods of achieving both of these objectives in order to be free of fear and able to enjoy the lives we were born to live.

TRUST

The single most important element that we can use to banish fear is TRUST. Trust is the antidote to fear, worry and doubt. However, it is a skill that we need to master if it is to work for us at its fullest potential.

Implicit within trust is the understanding that the Universe takes care of us at all times, that everything we need and want is presented to us in the perfect moment, that we are safe and secure, that we are guided to and given every opportunity to live at our highest potential, that every challenge or obstacle in our way is a gift and provides us with a forum for learning and growth and that our natural state is to be abundant, happy, loving and at peace.

Trust knows that if a job, relationship, baby or move is not forthcoming then it is not right for us at this time. Trust is in complete harmony with the rhythm and flow of life. It knows that nothing that cannot be replaced is ever lost and that no one can do anything to us that we do not allow. It knows that ultimately there is only love in the world and that everything that is not born of love is an illusion that we do not have to buy into and manifest.

It is clear that when we are living all these principles, there cannot be any possibility for fear to play any part in our lives. It is not enough to simply know these things in theory, they have to be put into action and this will take practice.

Part of the process of bringing trust into our being involves awareness. We need to see where our thoughts, words and actions are buying into fear and reinforcing the negative beliefs that we manifest as our reality.

1) Look at the list of common fears in part 1 and note which ones are predominant in your life.
2) What do you actively do to avoid dealing with these fears? How does this limit your life?
3) Are you being or doing something you do not enjoy because of fear?
4) Are you on course for the highest potential life that you were born to live?

INSTATING TRUST.

1) Become aware of your thoughts and feelings.
2) Every time you find yourself feeling fearful or are worrying or doubting yourself, have a trust statement to hand. These could be things like:
I TRUST I HAVE EVERY THING I NEED AND WANT IN THE PERFECT MOMENT.

RELEASING FEAR

I TRUST I AM SAFE AT ALL TIMES.
I TRUST THAT I AM TAKEN CARE OF AT ALL TIMES.
I TRUST MY LIFE IS PERFECT JUST AS IT IS.

3)   Don't just wait for fear to present itself before bringing in trust. Make it part of your daily ritual. In the morning look at the day ahead and inject trust into it. This may be to trust that everything that is meant to happen does, that the timing for every-thing is perfect even if you or someone else is late for an appointment, it is for a good reason. Look for the gifts and opportunities that will be presented and take full advantage of them. Have no precon-ceived ideas or expectations about this day, wait and see what turns up. If this is done, it will often pre-empt any fear, anger, hurt and guilt.

4)   In the early days of instating trust, you may feel as if you are just paying lip service to the concept. This is fine. Gradually the sense of trust will sink deeper into the conscious and unconscious until it becomes part of your being and is as natural as breathing.

5)   Trust is a muscle that needs to be exercised on a regular basis. It is not enough to do it once in a blue moon when you remember. Commit yourself to bringing in trust. Once you do, the immediate rewards are so great that they provide the impetus to carry on.

6)   Trust never looks to a specific outcome or to control anything. Know that whatever happens is the right thing for now. Create a win for yourself no matter what.

SURRENDER

Surrender can be quite an emotive word. In our society it implies giving up and losing the battle. The truth could not be further from this. Surrender is a very powerful tool that can be very effective in banishing fear on many different levels.

1)   Surrender is the best way we have of dealing with struggle. When we are battling to keep our

heads above water and swimming against the tide, we can stop and surrender. The ego will tell us that if we do this, we will drown and be destroyed. When we are fixated on a goal and we are struggling to attain it, it will probably not be the right destination. If this is the case, we were never going to get there or we would find it very unsatisfying if we did. When we surrender, we have no idea where this is going to take us, it is the journey that becomes more important. Fun, growth and fulfilment are built into the package. We wait to see what presents itself and decide if that option feels right for us.

a)   When you become aware that you are in struggle mode, **STOP.**

b)   Consciously surrender and give up the battle.

c)   Go with the flow and see where it takes you. This can be done in small ways as well as large ones. For instance, if you are stuck in traffic and are late for an appointment. Instead of railing against everything, getting uptight and trying to gain every inch, SURRENDER. There is nothing you can do but go with the flow of the traffic and use the time to relax or put on your favourite music or think up a new creative scheme. Trust that whenever you arrive at your destination will be ideal for everyone involved. Even if you have to cancel your plans there will be a gift attached. Surrender allows you to see and experience the gift.

2)   Use surrender when there is a big or stressful situation looming ahead. This could be anything from a job interview, a move, a divorce, exam or work deadline. There will often be a great deal of fear or worry focussed around this issue and it may completely dominate your life. When this occurs:-

a)   Catch the fear or worry and **STOP.**

b)   Surrender the situation to the higher part of yourself. You are in effect giving over control to the Divine aspect of yourself.

c)   Instate trust into the situation, knowing that the right outcome will ensue.

d)   Flow with the situation as and when it occurs and look to find the synchronicity and miracles that happen to get you through. If you surrender and trust they will always be there.

3)   Use surrender when you are in the midst of a fearful situation. This could be something like falling off a ladder. As you are in mid fall, you can bring in fear, which would tense up the body and create an injury. Equally you could surrender. This would relax the body, you go with the fall rather than try to control it and consequently any damage will be minimised. This is a technique I learned doing stage falls and I am sure many a stunt man would confirm it.

Another example of using surrender within a fearful situation happened to me. I was in a potential car crash, a car was coming straight for me at speed. I took evasive action and consequently lost control of the car. I remember surrendering and knowing that whatever the outcome of this situation, I would be able to deal with it. There were no consequences as it happened, I was unhurt, the car was not marked and the help I needed to extricate myself was there instantly.

RELEASING FEAR

When in a fearful situation:-

a)   Instate surrender BEFORE the fear has a chance to kick in.

b)   Relax and hand over the consequences of the situation to a higher part of yourself.

c)   Stay in the moment and only deal with what is and not what might be.

ACCEPTANCE

Acceptance is another powerful means of combating fear. When we are in a complete state of acceptance, we are at one with who we are, the situations we find ourselves in and everyone else around us. There is no room for fear when we accept everything just as it is.

1)   Constantly choose to accept every aspect of life, just as it is.

2)   As circumstances change, allow the acceptance to change with them.

STAYING IN THE MOMENT

Fear is always about the future and not the present. Even when we are in a fearful situation, it is usually the consequences of it that we worry or are fearful about.

The ego works with and through the mind and it is usually here that the illusions of fear are created. If we have a great deal of time where the mind is given free rein, fears can be manufactured out of nothing.

In dealing with fear, it is necessary to discipline the mind to stay in the present and not to slip into speculation about a future that does not yet exist. When fear comes in, our attention needs to be brought back into this moment.

1)   When you feel fear, **STOP.**

2)   Take the focus of attention out of the mind and onto the outside world. Consciously notice things that are there only for this moment. A fly buzzing at the window, a leaf blowing in the wind, the words of a song on the radio. It doesn't matter what it is as

long as you give it 100% of your attention. Your ego will try to pull you back into the fear so be strong.

3)   Use a trust affirmation repeatedly to block any other fear thoughts from getting in.

4)   Take some deep breaths to calm the body and to stop the physical fear response.

5)   Focus on this moment and begin to acknowledge all the positives.

In this moment I am safe.

In this moment I have enough food, shelter, and clothes.

In this moment I am loved.

In this moment I am enough.

In this moment I have friends.

In this moment I have gifts, talents and abilities that can be put to good use.

6)   Nothing else exists out of this present moment. The past is gone and the future is being created out of the thoughts, words and actions that you are putting out IN THIS MOMENT. You do not

want to project fear and manifest it in your future.

DEALING WITH THE
"WHAT IFS..."

When the "what if" train pulls into the station in our minds, we have to make sure that we do not hop on and allow it to take us to the depths of fear at the end of the line. We can jump off the train of thought at any point along the way but it is far better to learn not to get on board in the first place.

Remember that "what ifs" are fed to us by the ego and are ALWAYS an illusion.

1) Begin to become conscious and aware of your thoughts in order to catch a "what if" in its infancy.

2) As soon as you notice a "what if" intruding on the mind, have a visual tool to hand. See yourself squashing it underfoot like a bug or laugh at it and throw it in the rubbish bin or see it on a piece of paper with you setting light to it. Breathe the fear

out of the system as you do this.

3)   If you only catch the "what if" once it has grown to a fear, **STOP.** Do not allow the thought to go any further.

4)   Take back the power and energy that you have already unconsciously given to the fear. See it shrinking as a result. Laugh at the situation and yourself for having allowed it to get this far.

5)   Breathe out any emotions that may have arisen as a result of this. Fear, anger, pain, hurt or guilt are the main culprits.

6)   Bring yourself back to "WHAT IS", especially in relationship to the particular area of life that the "what if" dealt with.

7)   Remember that it requires the discipline to do this every time a "what if" appears. If you do so, they will occur less and less and will appear to be more ludicrous when they do. The ego knows your vulnerable and weak areas and will tend to target them when feeding you your "what ifs".

BREATHING

The breath is an incredibly powerful tool that we have at our disposal and we can use it in two different ways when dealing with fear.

First, we can use the breath to deactivate the fear response in the body. When we breathe too shallowly, we send a message to the brain that we are in danger and this will often set off the fight or flight response. The fact is that very few of us know how to breathe properly and consequently we are stressed and tired. Deep breathing activates a feel good response, we are relaxed, the body is able to heal itself, the added oxygen will feed the brain and aid concentration. We feel and are more positive and happy. The benefits to deeper breathing are endless. If we bring more breath into the body, we will find that there is less fear, worry and stress as a matter of course.

The second useful way in which we can use the breath to help combat fear is to use it to expel any fear that arises. The emotional feeling of fear is a tangible energy. We will find it in the solar plexus region of the body. We use the breath as a shovel. It goes down and picks up some of this destructive energy and it is then forcibly expelled from the body, it then goes down for another load until the feeling is no longer there. Nothing could be more simple or effective.

1)   Bring deeper breathing into every day life.
Take time each day to breathe consciously. This does not have to become a chore. It can be done in the car or while travelling, while waiting in a queue or in bed last thing at night or first thing in the morning. You could put post it notes up to remind you. Get into a habit of deeper breathing and notice the difference in how you feel as a result.
2)   If you are going into a stressful or fearful situation like a job interview or a hospital or dental procedure, use it before during and after. Focussing on the breath will also take the attention away from

the mind and therefore the fear.

3)   Whenever you feel fear, use the breath to expel it. Sometimes fear may occur when you think back to a time in your life when you have had a difficult time. When this happens, use the opportunity to release the fear that was created at that time.

USING YOUR INTUITION

The best defence we have against finding ourselves in situations that would create fear is our intuition. This amazing part of ourselves not only steers and guides us towards the positive things in our lives, but also protects us from the negative ones. If we listen to and act upon our intuition, we need never experience anything untoward.

An example of this happened to me. I was driving on the fast lane of a motorway and I noticed that the middle lane was free so I went to move across. An inner voice told me to stay where I was and the car stayed in the fast lane even as I tried to move over. I acknowledged the message and then tried to look for a reason for the warning. There was a juggernaut opposite me in the slow lane but there was nothing in front of it so it would have no reason to come out. Just then the lorry veered out into the middle lane where I would have been well and truly squashed. There are countless similar stories that people tell about how they missed trains or planes that crashed.

It is essential that we build up a relationship with our intuition so that information can be clearly given and received to keep us safe and stress free at all times. The ego mind will always try and negate any information that we get from the intuition. If we let logic talk us out of any pre-emptive action, we will regret it. Intuition that is not acted upon will always result in negative consequences.

1)   Connect with your intuition on a regular basis.

2)   Have an awareness of the difference between the intuitive voice and the ego voice. The ego will warn you against things in a way that creates fear

instead of warding it off. The intuitive voice is often a gut feeling that does not engender any fear. The ego will limit you while the intuition will set you free.

3)   Be aware of the gut feelings you have about people, whether they are worthy of your trust or not. Sometimes we have nothing to go on other than our instinct. We can avoid a great deal of pain and unnecessary anguish, simply by listening to our intuition and not getting involved with those who will create problems for us.

4)   When you get an intuitive feeling or sign, do not ignore it or let the ego talk you out of it.

5)   Always act upon the communication. You may not be given any reason for the feeling, so this takes a great deal of trust.

DEALING WITH PANIC ATTACKS

1)   Have the commitment and intention to deal with this debilitating condition.

2)   Look at the pay-offs that having this condition creates. What are you afraid of that this acts as a buffer to? It may be success, failure, intimacy, rejection, being independent or many other common fears. If you are not willing to give up the pay-offs, you will sabotage any healing that may be done.

3)   Do any other members of your family have this condition? If so what influence has this had on you?

4)   Look at the places and situations you avoid in case you have an attack. Make a list of these. Acknowledge the degree to which this limits you. Do you have attacks if other people are with you or only on your own?

5)   Learn the slow breathing techniques and use this as a means of warding off any attacks. Practice

the breathing on a regular basis.

6)   Take up yoga, t'ai chi or chi gong as these will help the body to cope.

7)   Begin to gently introduce yourself into "no go" places or situations. Get support but do not become dependant on it. Prepare yourself in advance with the breathing and affirming that you are safe at all times.

8)   Take your attention away from yourself and your physical symptoms. If you are waiting for the feelings to appear, you can end up creating them. Use whatever means you need to distract yourself, sing a song, read a book, recite the alphabet or anything that takes the emphasis away from your panic.

9)   If the panic does set in, make an effort to use the breath to forcibly expel the fear from the body. This is helpful anyway as the feeling of not being able to breathe is often due to the fact that the lungs are full and you are trying to take in more air.

If you breathe out, the in breath becomes automatic.
10)   Tap the fear out of the physical body. The two main fear release areas are just below the eyes and on the side of the hands about three quarters of an inch below the little finger. Keep tapping firmly in these areas until the fear feelings subside.
11)   Gradually work through all your trigger areas, disconnecting from any attachments to the fear.
12)   Work on finding out the unconscious sources of the fears and eliminating them. (see process).
13)   Reward yourself for any progress that is made

and do not give up if there are set backs.

FEAR AND NEED

Behind most fears that we have, there is often an unfulfilled need lurking. When the fears are born out of need, it may be necessary to address that particular need in order to heal and release the fear. For instance, a need for approval and praise that is not filled may create a fear of judgement, criticism or ridicule. A need to be loved that is not consistently met can manifest fears of rejection, abandonment and not being good enough.

Most of our needs and consequently the fears that are associated with them are created in childhood. A need in an adult is some thing that we did not receive with any reliability as a child. When we are grown up, no matter how much of that thing we are given, it is never enough. Need becomes a bottomless pit that cannot be filled.

It stands to reason that if we actively work on releasing and fulfiling our own needs, then the illusions of fear will dissipate.

One of the best ways to find out what our personal needs are is to look at our expectations within a relationship. We will usually look to a partner to meet our needs.

1)   Make a list of your needs whether fulfilled or unfulfilled.
2)   What fears have been created out of these?

3)   Who or what circumstances created these needs in childhood? i.e. An abusive or neglectful parent, a divorce, illness or death of a family member.

4)   Who do you get to try and meet these needs as an adult or do you suppress them rather than face disappointment?

5)   Do you attract people and situations that simply reinforce your fears?

DISARMING THE EGO

The most important positive role that the ego plays in our lives is to show us the unhealed fear illusions that are hidden or buried in our unconscious. Fear is the main weapon the ego has to use. In releasing our fears, we disarm the ego until it has no armoury and consequently no power to affect us. At this point, we are set free to live our lives unhindered by debilitating fears.

The disarming process is a long term one and

can only be done as and when the fears are brought to our attention.

1)   Be aware of your feelings.
2)   Remember that fear shows itself in many different guises such as anger, hurt, guilt, jealousy and shame.
3)   If you have a strong fear like not being good enough, it may present itself in many different ways. Each of these may need to be dealt with separately.
4)   As soon as you become aware of a strong feeling, look at what happened to trigger it. Was it something someone said, a situation, a visual trigger or an old memory that came into your mind on a particular train of thought? This needs to be done as soon as possible after the awareness kicks in. Some of the triggers are very subtle and can pass through your consciousness very quickly.
5)   See if you can remember what this trigger relates back to. It may be that the source is hidden

deeper in the unconscious.

6)   Release any emotion that has arisen by forcibly expelling it on the breath. Do this until the feeling is no longer there.

7)   Take all the information gathered and use it in the process for releasing the fear.

RELEASING AND REMOVING FEAR

Ultimately the only way to completely remove fear from our lives is to go to the places where it was created in the first place. As I have already stated, the fear is born out of the experiences that we have had and how we chose to perceive them at the time. We will create a programme complete with beliefs about ourselves and the world, which then become part of the fear. There may also be byproducts of fear like anger, guilt or hurt that also attach themselves to the fear and the experience. These all become lodged in the unconscious as a package that may be triggered and brought to the surface at any time. It is imperative that we release all these aspects if we are to be completely free of fear.

There may have been many reinforcements of our fears along the way and it is important not to mistake them for the source. If the fear was already present during the situation IT IS NOT THE SOURCE. It will be necessary to release the fear from the various layers that have repeated and increased the fear. For instance, we may have a fear of public speaking. This may have shown itself as an adult when we had to give a presentation or lead a meeting and we made a mess of it. There may have been a couple of incidents in school where we had to stand up in front of the class and froze even though we knew the answers or material. We may have forgotten our lines in a school play or been laughed at when we got it wrong. None of these things will be the source but they will need to be released along the way. Each experience will have strengthened and reinforced the fear.

At each layer we clear, we need to ask the unconscious if this is the source. In many cases we may have to go further back than this life to find the true source.

THE PROCESS

1)   Look at the fear or situation that has been brought to your attention NOW. What beliefs and feelings are attached to it? Write these down so you don't forget.

2)   Look back in your conscious memory and note how many times you have found yourself in similar situations or experiencing the same feelings. How old were you at the time? What were the circumstances surrounding it etc?

3)   The first stage of the process will be to clear the conscious layers of the fear starting with the most recent from the conscious and unconscious.

4)   The feelings will be the first thing to release.

RELEASING FEAR

There will usually be other emotions as well as fear within each situation. These may be humiliation, shame, anger, hurt, guilt, jealousy and pain. These are forcibly breathed out and away from the body.

5)   You will also want to look at and release the beliefs and thoughts that you took on at the time. These will be things like "I am not good enough.", "If I let people get close, I will be hurt.", "I am not safe.", "People want to hurt and destroy me.", "If I dare to be myself, I will be judged and criticised for it." And many more. These beliefs alone are enough to create the reality. When we release the situation and the beliefs it is like ejecting a video or a floppy disc containing the computer programme. We are removing that particular programme from our memory banks.

6)   Once a memory along with the fears and beliefs are removed from the unconscious, we need to replace them with a positive scenario. This can be seeing the gift that the situation was there to provide or coming through the challenge victorious, having learned the lesson and without any negative

residue. You can programme this and the good feelings attached to it by placing this new video or disc in the memory banks instead of the one you have released.

7)   Each time you do this, you lighten the load that you are carrying of heavy fears and beliefs.

8)   The layers of fear that are not in our conscious memory going back to the source can be dealt with next. It is important to note that the source is often very small, especially compared to the later manifestations. A fear will often feed off itself and grow out of all proportion. The source in childhood may be an incident that to an adult would not be significant. For instance, a child may be waiting excitedly for its father to come home from work, when he does he is tired, stressed and short tempered. The child feels hurt and rejected and out of this a fear of these things is born.

9)   The way to find out what is in the unconscious is simply to ask it. To do this there are two things we need. First, to be relaxed enough to hear the

answers and secondly to quieten the ego so that it cannot block or sabotage the process. To do both of these we need to breathe deeply and take all the focus away from the mind and put it onto the body and the solar-plexus. The answers come as a feeling or sense of knowing rather than a clear voice. Every time we get a reply the ego will try to put doubt in our way and if we allow it, we lose the connection.

10)   In working with the unconscious it will help to work with the questions on tape or ask a friend to ask them. Keep the questions simple with a either/or or yes/no reply so that we do not have to engage the mind too much.

11)   For each unconscious layer you want to find out

a)   The circumstances.

b)   The feelings generated.

c)   The belief systems created.

Rememberr that when you get to the source, the fear will only emerge as a result of the situation.

a)   Establish what age you were. Ask the unconscious if you were under five, under four etc.

b)　　Locate the incident. Was it at home, someone else's home, a public place, inside or outside? Which room were you in?

c)　　Find out the time of day or night.

d)　　Who else was there at the time?

e)　　Was the situation created out of what was said to you, done to you or witnessed?

f)　　What feelings came up as a result?

g)　　What beliefs were created?

h)　　How did the situation end up?

12)　Breathe out any feelings or emotions attached to the situation.

13)　Eject the whole scenario from the unconscious mind and memory bank. See a video emerge and pull out the tape so that it cannot play again.

14)　Reprogram the same scenario but allow your adult self to reassure, comfort and explain to the child an understanding that does not include any fear, guilt, hurt etc. Instill good feelings and positive beliefs in the child and how to deal with any similar situations that may occur in future. EMPOWER the child.

15)   Push this new programme back down into the unconscious mind and memory banks.

16)   Ask the unconscious mind if this is the source of the fear. If the answer is no, then repeat the process on the next layer and so on.

17)   If the source goes back into a past life, the process is similar, the questions will be slightly different.

(If past lives do not fit in with your personal belief system then ignore the following process)

a)   Are you male or female?

b)   Do you live in an urban or rural area?

c)   Do you come from a rich, poor or in-between background?

d)   What time of life did the situation creating the fear occur? Were you a child, adolescent, young adult, middle aged or old aged?

e)   What era was this? More than 200 years, more than 500, more than 1,000?

f)   What family do you have?

g)   What were the circumstances that created the incident?

h)   Who was involved?

i)   What feelings and beliefs were created out of the situation?

18) When the scenario has emerged, eject and release everything from this point on within that lifetime.

19)   In reprogramming the lifetime, replace the circumstances with those that would occur in an ideal world, without losing any of the lessons or gifts that were there.

20)   Make sure you leave a good feeling behind before bringing the focus of attention back into this moment.

NB It is safe to do this process as you are not reliving the past experience but finding out about it and releasing any residue that is not serving you.

TIPS FOR DEALING WITH FEAR

TRUST - Anytime fear, worry or doubt emerges, instate trust. It is the antidote.

STAY IN THE MOMENT - Focus your attention on what is and not what might be.

BREATHE - Learn to deepen the breath to calm the body and the mind.

FEAR IS AN ILLUSION - it only becomes real when you believe it and manifest it.

BRING IN THE LIGHT - Fear is the dark, shadow side of ourselves. Surround yourself with light to dispel the shadow.

FEAR IS A CHOICE - We can choose not to be fearful or have it play a part in your life.

FEAR IS THE INVERSION OF LOVE - To remove any fear, simply ask yourself "What would love do?"

FIND THE SOURCE - Find the place that created the initial illusion and choose to see it differently.

RELEASING FEAR

GO WITH THE FLOW - Surrender and give over control to a higher power and flow with the rhythm of life.

FLIP THE COIN OVER - When you feel fear, choose to change the label on the feeling to excitement and anticipation for what lies ahead.

SET YOURSELF FREE - Commit yourself to the removal of fear in your life and you will be free forever.

I wish you a life free of fear and its side effects.

LIZ ADAMSON.

Liz Adamson is available for one to one sessions, talks and workshops.
Contact: Flat 3, Hamptons, Hadlow, Tonbridge, Kent, TN11 9SR.
E-mail. liz@edenbook.co.uk
Tel 07940 101918

**OPTIMAL LIVING PUBLICATIONS
FOR INFO OR ORDERS
CALL 01732 810430**
WWW.OPTIMALLIVINGINSTITUTE.CO.U

Available by Liz Adamson

The Ultimate Guides to Emotional Freedom

Releasing Anger	£4.95
Releasing Hurt and Sadness	£4.95
Releasing Fear	£4.95
Releasing Guilt	£4.95
Embracing Happiness	£4.95
Embracing Love	£4.95

Overcoming Sexual and Childhood Abuse
£7.95

Overcoming Weight Issues   £7.95
Subliminal Weight Tape or CD

12 Principles of Optimal Living   £7.95

Relationships   £7.95

Abundance and Prosperity   £7.95

DVD
Past Lives with Liz Adamson   £14.95

Secrets of Optimal Living Cards   £7.95

All above titles soon to be available on high quality CD and Tape.